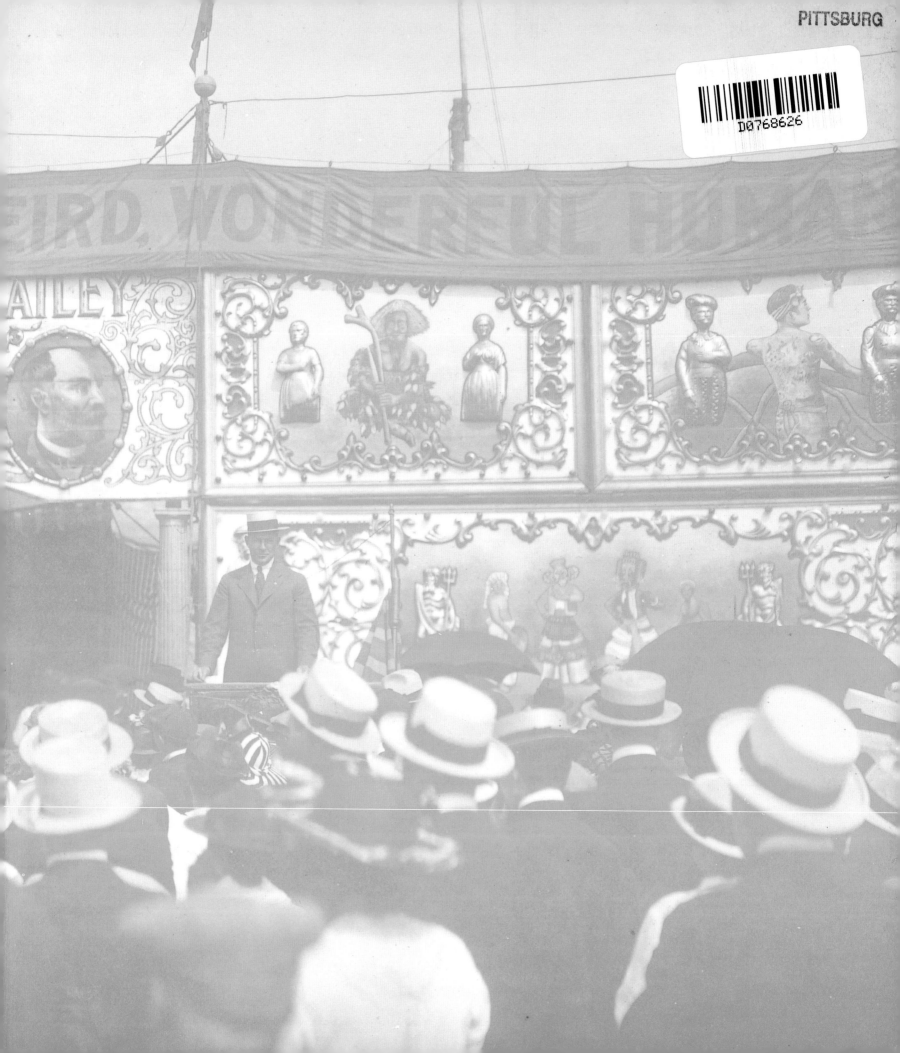

WILD, WEIRD, AND WONDERFUL

OTHER BOOKS BY THE AUTHOR

Hoaxes, Humbugs, and Spectacles:
Astonishing Photographs of Smelt Wrestlers, Human Projectiles,
Giant Hailstones, Contortionists, Elephant Impersonators, and Much, Much More!
(co-authored with Roger Manley and Michelle Van Parys)

Dear Mr. Ripley: A Compendium of Curioddities from the Believe It Or Not! *Archives*
(co-authored with Roger Manley and Michelle Van Parys)

Self-Made Worlds: Visionary Folk Art Environments
(co-authored with Roger Manley)

The Rarest of the Rare: Stunning Specimens at the Harvard Museum of Natural History
(co-authored with Nancy Pick)

WILD, WEIRD, AND WONDERFUL

The American Circus 1901-1927
As seen by F.W. Glasier, Photographer

BY
Mark Sloan

Introduction by
Timothy Tegge

A Project of the META Museum
The Quantuck Lane Press, New York

The value of any object that supplies the wants and pleasures of mankind is compounded of its substance and form, of the materials and the manufacture. Its price must depend on the number of persons by whom it may be acquired and used; on the extent of the market; and consequently on the ease or difficulty of remote exportation, according to the nature of the commodity, its local situation, and the temporary circumstances of the world.

Edward Gibbon
The Decline and Fall of the Roman Empire

❮ SELLS FLOTO BIG TOP, BROCKTON, MA, 1923

Originally known as the Great Floto Dog & Pony Show, the Sells Floto Circus began operations in 1902. The circus was owned and operated by Harry H. Tammen and Fred G. Bonfils, who also owned the *Denver Post*. The show was named after Otto Floto, a sports writer with the paper. Willie Sells (of Sells Bros. Circus fame) joined as general director of the show in 1906. When the Buffalo Bill & Pawnee Bill combined show went bankrupt in 1913, Tammen and Bonfils immediatley hired Buffalo Bill Cody as a headline attraction for their 1914 season. Cody spent the next few seasons (through 1916) with the show. He died in 1917. Tammen and Bonfils finally sold the Sells Floto show in its entirety to Muggivan, Bowers and Ballard (American Circus Corporation) of Peru, Indiana, in 1920.

A WORLD OF WONDERS

The photographs of Fred Whitman Glasier could be favorably compared to a great cross section of rock and debris cutting the ancient earth at an archaeological site. At first glance, they seem to represent a single, very important slice (1901–27) of circus history. This in itself is significant enough. But, on closer inspection, one discovers the human drama behind the circus, which runs much deeper than the sparkle of its costumes and the excitement of its feats.

From its earliest incarnation to today's modern day spectacle, the circus has been an important part of America's heritage, a legacy deeply rooted in rich cultures gathered from around the globe. The components of the circus can be traced to early civilization. The first recorded evidence of juggling, for example, can be found in tomb paintings dating back four thousand years. They depict groups of Egyptians tossing balls in the air. Early Etruscan frescos portray entertainers balancing objects on their heads while musicians play flute-like instruments. Details from Ancient Greek vases illustrate such scenes as gymnastic leaps on horses' backs and female acrobats performing handstands. Tumblers, rope-walkers, stilt-walkers and jesters amused the Greco-Roman world for many centuries and, in time, trained animals, from dogs, monkeys, and bears to numerous exotic beasts, were also presented for entertainment. As early as 275 B.C., Romans witnessed performances by elephants.

During the early days of imperial Rome, an elliptical, roofless stadium with seating for over 250,000 spectators was built to accommodate chariot races, gladiator events, and acrobatic and equestrian exhibitions. Frequently, these great spectacles would begin with an opening procession of horses and chariots, men and beasts. These events were called the Circus Maximus, often considered to be the actual beginning of circus itself. The popularity of these Roman events was substantial enough to necessitate construction of several additional amphitheaters throughout the empire, smaller but nonetheless massive in size. Among them were the famous Coliseum and Circus Flaminius. Whereas crowds cheered on the proficient equestrians and gymnasts, the core attractions offered were "to-the-death" battles between men and wild animals. After the fall of the Roman empire in the fifth century A.D., the great majority of amphitheaters were left to deteriorate. The vast spectacles disappeared completely and what remained at the beginning of the medieval period was a scattered assortment of horsemen and artists with no formal arena to perform in. It is probable that a diversity of performance skills were passed down through the generations that followed.

Thirteenth-century Egyptian marketplaces exhibited conjurers and hand-balancers, men who swallowed swords, and animal hypnotists possessing seemingly supernatural powers over everything from snakes to lions. At the same time, minstrels roamed Europe telling stories, singing songs, presenting puppet shows, and often displaying feats of acrobatics for the townspeople. Jugglers, jesters, tightrope walkers, strong men, and dancing bears entertained on street corners and occasionally in castles and palaces. Such presentations continued through the medieval era. By the 1600s country fairs had gained popularity throughout England and soon featured animal training and feats of agility.

In the mid-1700s, a more recognizable form of circus took shape. It began on horseback with a small handful of accomplished riders in England. These enterprising men would charter a field near a public house or tea garden, rope off a designated area, and publicize an exhibition. Viewers watched in amazement as the able equestrians straddled two or three horses, moving with precision at breakneck speed. About this time, Philip Astley, a former sergeant-major in the British Light Dragoons, left the army and took a job as a groom at one of these English riding academies. It was here that he observed, practiced and eventually perfected many of the moves executed by his instructors. In 1768 he opened his own riding school and show grounds in London. Astley is credited with discovering that centrifugal force held a person on the back of a horse as it galloped in a circle. This discovery led to his development of the first circus ring, which, after some experimentation, Astley decided should have a diameter of 42 feet. It is also believed among historians that he is responsible for creating the first-ever clown entree in circus history, a routine in which a clown cannot seem to mount his horse. When finally he gets on the horse, the animal refuses to budge—until not only does it bump the comedian off its back, but chases him out of the arena. This was added into the show as early as 1769. As the next several years passed, Astley inserted acts with dogs and ducks, tumblers, equilibrists, and other novelties. Within a ten-year period, his equestrian achievements and showmanship had won him significant acclaim. By 1780, Astley had fenced in his show grounds, adding proper seats and a roof for the comfort of his audience. It is no surprise, then, that Philip Astley is recognized as the inventor of the modern circus.

In America, itinerant showmen who performed for the settlers have been documented as early as 1724. Tight-and slack-rope artists, jugglers, clowns, puppeteers, trick riders, and smaller performing animals such as dogs, monkeys, and birds independently appeared on street corners and in town squares, much as they had been doing abroad for centuries. However, it wasn't until April 3, 1793, that the first actual circus opened on American soil. John Bill Ricketts introduced this exciting new concept first, in Philadelphia. Ricketts was a Scottish equestrian who served apprenticeship in London under one of Astley's major riding school competitors, Charles Hughes. He constructed a wooden amphitheater at Twelfth and Market Streets to house his show, which, like Astley's before him, featured generous offerings of trick riding, acrobatics, clown pantomimes, and rope walkers. Less than a few short weeks into its inaugural engagement, the Ricketts Circus was attended not once, but twice by President George and Martha Washington. With the President's approval of this new entertainment enterprise, the circus was assured immense success. The show finished its Philadelphia run on July 22nd and Rickets moved his troupe to New York, where he built another arena for a three-month stand. Every time the circus relocated, a new structure needed to be constructed. In time, several circus buildings existed in the eastern United States. And before too long, new circus proprietors entered the ranks of showmen. The American circus had been successfully established.

Though often referred to as permanent, many of the early circus buildings were nothing more than an open-air lot surrounded by a wooden shell. They were permanent only in the sense that they were not movable. When business in any given city began to drop off, the show proprietor would sell his building for scrap and move on. Around 1822 the American traveling menageries, with cages full of exotic animals, had taken to the roads, growing considerably in size and popularity. To be certain that consumers couldn't see their precious cargo without first purchasing admission, management erected canvas sidewalls to enclose their wagons—indeed a clever idea. In 1825 Joshua Purdy Brown, an ingenious showman from Somers, New York, revolutionized the American circus by presenting his show under a tent. From this point forward, circuses could erect their big top in any size community, stay for one day or several, take it down, pack it into wagons and move overnight to a new town. Circuses could now explore new territories, reaching smaller communities that had never been exposed to its wonders before. This single innovation marked the birth of what would soon become an institution—the Great American Traveling Circus.

The early wagon, or "mud," shows are a fine illustration of the resilience of the circus. Wagon shows traveled over dirt and gravel roads at the pace of horses walking, in any kind of weather—heat, cold, wind, rain. A fifteen-mile trip from town to town could take all night if the path was rutted or muddy. Wagons were constantly getting stuck in the mire and axles would break from sudden drops into deep holes. The trip could only be as predictable as the weather, condition of the terrain, or disposition of the horses. After a long day—which usually began before dawn with setting up the tents, then parading, presenting two shows, tearing down and loading up again—those driving the wagons overland could endanger themselves, passengers, and cargo by falling asleep, hypnotized by the slow swaying back and forth of the wagon and the rumble and clanking of the caravan in motion. It was a hard, rugged way of life, but these troupers paved the way for many others who would someday follow in their tracks, and their way of life continued through and beyond the Civil War.

The country continued to grow. Towns became cities, which blossomed into metropolises. Roads remained treacherous, particularly in the more remote portions of the states, but they too had noticeably improved. Some circuses traversed the waterways as a means to expand their itineraries. Wagonloads of equipment, animals, and personnel would be loaded onto a riverboat or barge and cruise from one location to the next. Once the boat docked, the show would roll off the vessel, move to a nearby lot, and circus day would begin. In fact, it was one such riverboat circus that first caught the eye of the five young brothers Ringling when it journeyed down the Mississippi in the late 1860s. Circuses prospered with the expansion of the United States. There were countless shows roaming the country during this period, many of them quite substantial. Some became so large that it was no longer profitable for them to play smaller cities on their routes. The completion of the first transcontinental railroad in 1869 provided a groundbreaking solution for the visionary showmen—the circus must be put on rails.

Dan Costello's circus was the first to make a transcontinental jump by rail. His trek west began within days of the driving of the Golden Spike. But he was not the first circus man to move a show using the railroads. In fact, the Stone & Madigan Circus moved intermittently on rails through the Mississippi Valley as early as 1851. Once Costello took his giant step, however, others followed suit. And so it was that, in 1872, legendary showman

Phineas Taylor Barnum framed his first railroad circus with the expertise of Dan Costello and William Cameron Coup. Coup is awarded credit for inventing the unique and efficient crossover plate, a device that changed the method in which all railroad circus flatcars were loaded from 1872 on. This system is still in use today with the modern Ringling Bros. and Barnum & Bailey train. By the turn of the twentieth century, there were at least twenty different shows riding the steel rails across an ever-expanding US. Now circuses could claim specific territories for themselves. The railroad circus giants of the day, such as Barnum & Bailey and Ringling Bros. (both separate entities until their combination in 1919), Forepaugh & Sells, and John Robinson, to name a few, built their routes around stops in major city markets, while the remaining wagon shows—and there were still plenty of them—continued to show in smaller towns and cities not accessible by rail. The circus had conquered America and was definitely in its heyday.

It may be difficult for someone today to imagine the magnitude of the circus between 1900 and 1920. One-hundred-car trains, split into four sections and loaded with everything imaginable, snaked their way across the map for eight months, spilling out shows so monumental that, on circus day, businesses shut down early and schools closed. In many localities, it was the second most important day of the year—Christmas being the first. It became a ritual to set out for the rail yards at dawn to watch these monstrous trains unload. Many followed the stream of animals and wagons to the lot and watched the show come to life. By mid-morning, anything circus that could walk, ride, or trot prepared for a street parade. This is where "towners," as they were called, got their first look at the contents of great cage wagons and flashy wardrobe, or heard the shrill pierce of a calliope. This procession also put the finishing touches on an advertising campaign, which billposting crews began weeks ahead of time. Giant posters in lush colors had foretold the wonders that would appear in town, usually for one day only. And here they were, finally—parading down Main Street. Of course, after staring at posters on every barnside, fence, or window for weeks, then being teased by this free spectacle, hardly a person could resist the lure of the circus. Town folk lined up at ticket wagons by the scores, the calculated payoff to a job well done by the advertising department.

A bird's-eye view of a circus lot during its heyday was a sight almost impossible to believe. When posters proclaimed "a city of canvas" or "acres of tents," they were not exaggerating. First, there was the midway—an open-air tunnel of sorts, lined on one side with larger-than-life canvas banners depicting "strange and unusual people, gathered from the four corners of the earth." Behind these fabric paintings stood the sideshow tent. Directly across were ticket wagons and concession wagons, serving up exotic cuisine like cotton candy and "frozen delight." There were pony ride tops and maybe a "pit show," a separate attraction of snakes or giant lizards. Some circuses even included a free aerial act on the midway to tempt patrons into arriving on the grounds early to spend more money. Down the middle of this runway were souvenir stands along with balloon and program salesmen. And straight ahead, the main entrance—the threshold to another world.

Once through the marquee, patrons found themselves in the menagerie, surrounded by cage wagons housing rare and exotic animals. There were elephants, camels, rhinos, and more. The menagerie, at last, carried them into the largest tent on the show grounds, the big top. This is where the actual performance unfurled. During the golden age, the time the photographs in this book were taken, the big top alone was larger than a football field. It had to be. It covered three rings, four stages, a wide track which divided the front row seats from the rings, and had seating for ten thousand people. It has been said that if you sat at one end of the big top for the matinee and the opposite for the evening show, you would have seen an entirely different program at each location.

Behind the scenes, the circus backyard was its own city. There was the cookhouse—a restaurant, so to speak, where three full meals were prepared and served to fifteen hundred employees daily at no cost. If anyone craved a pack of cigarettes or other refreshments, a commissary wagon known as the "pie car" was available. Such indulgences were at the performer's expense. There was the "pad room," or canvassed stable, housing several hundred horses, and, next to it, a blacksmith shop. There was a barbershop and a doctor's office. Circuses even employed their own veterinarians. In short, circus management did its best to cover all bases. For instance, adults were allotted two buckets of water each day. With these rations, they could bathe or wash clothes. All contracted personnel, regardless of status, were provided with accommodations on the train. Though far from spacious in most cases, everyone had a place to sleep, store belongings, and be carried from city to city. Most importantly, every week at designated times staff members would congregate in line at the office, or "red wagon," to collect their salaries. Everyone with a circus put in long hours and worked hard for his or her money, from the workers to the headlining artistes. The pay scale spanned quite a range. In 1915, a porter on the Ringling Bros. Circus train received a salary of $3.75 per week. An "elephant man"—not a trainer, but a basic menagerie hand—received $5.00. On the opposite end of the spectrum, Ringling Bros.' renowned aerialist, Lillian Leitzel, brought home an extravagant $150.00 per week for her twice-daily appearances in the show. Leitzel was also allowed the rare privilege of being exempt from all street parades and production numbers—perks of stardom.

The circus lifestyle was, and still is, an extraordinary existence. For those involved, it is not about money, practicality, nor even necessarily fame or glory, but about something larger—a shared humanity, and all that goes along with it. The circus has always been a larger-than-life creature, showing up out of nowhere and then, as quickly and unexpectedly as it came, disappearing once again. The photographs in this collection mirror that creature in a time long gone. They speak in loud and distinctive voices, like the circus itself. The faces are haunting, the emotions are strong, and the vibrant colors of what the circus was and is still burst through the remarkable black and white illustrations included in these pages. Glasier's work is a testimony to the simple fact that, indeed, there is nothing else on earth quite like the circus.

Timothy Noel Tegge, June, 2002

Timothy Noel Tegge was born and raised in the circus. For twenty-five years, his family owned and operated a small one-ring show that traveled from coast to coast. Tegge began clowning at the age of three, signaling the beginning of a life-long love affair with the circus.

ADVANCE CREW, BARNUM & BAILEY CIRCUS, BROCKTON, MA 1906

By 1867 advertisers had already begun leasing space on the sides of buildings and fences. Bradbury and Houghteling of New York initiated a nationwide painting and posting service for advertisers. By 1870, nearly three hundred small sign-painting and bill-posting companies existed. Advance crew for the circus would usually precede the show by two weeks, often papering over previous or competing circus billboards.

FRED WHITMAN GLASIER
1865-1950

Fred Whitman Glasier was a commercial portrait photographer with a studio in Brockton, Massachusetts. He worked during a time when the approach to portrait photography was dictated by the conventions of portrait painting. Applying this standard, the public grew to expect portraits containing columns and balustrades and filled with luxurious accoutrements. In turn, studios competed to have more and more ornate sets on hand to serve as backdrops.

Glasier was no exception to this rule. He remained true, almost to the letter, to the conventions of the studio photographer and seems to have had a keen entrepreneurial ambition. He often sold portraits of popular celebrities out of the window of his studio, as was common at the time, and gave slide lectures on his photographed subjects. He claimed to be personally acquainted with P. T. Barnum, the Ringling Brothers, James Bailey, Adam Forepaugh, Sr., the Sells Brothers, and William F. Cody. Dropping names such as these must have contributed mightily to the success of his illustrated lectures. This proved doubly profitable due to the free advertising for both the prints and his studio which resulted from the presentations. Since several of the lectures on Native American and Western topics were quite popular, Glasier's claim of both Native American and of pioneer ancestry could be viewed as either the reason for his interest in the subject or perhaps a clever marketing ploy. Given an advertisement stating that he was "one of the first to venture into the field of High Speed Photography" and that he "made a success in this line that was thought to be practically impossible," Glasier's flair for self-promotion must be taken into account, as fast shutter speeds were not a rarity during his worklife. (It is interesting to note, however, that in a letter his wife mentions that he was adopted into the Massasoit tribe "by blood" by Miss Lottie Mitchell, the "last descendant of Massasoit, the Pilgrim's friend." There is a photo of one of Lottie Mitchell's sisters on page 62).

Glasier was born in 1865 in Adams, Massachusetts. He began his career as a textile designer before developing an infatuation with photography. In a leap from his successful studio practice, he first ventured to photograph circus performers in situ in 1896. The following collection, taken from 1901 to 1927, shows Glasier's work at a critical juncture, documenting his split from the tradition of strictly commercial photography. Though the circus was never short on hired promotional photographers, Glasier's approach proved novel. Unlike his contemporaries, he never traveled with the shows, but rather used the spectacle as convenient and interesting subject matter when it was at hand, taking publicity photos for the Barnum & Bailey, Adam Forepaugh, Sells Bros., Ringling Bros., and Sparks circuses when they came to his area. Due to his interest in the West, Glasier also photographed Buffalo Bill's Wild West Show and the 101 Real Wild West Show. Included in this collection is a photo of Chief Iron Tail, whose likeness was among those used in the design of the buffalo nickel (page 63).

Glasier focused exclusively on the performers rather than taking pictures of audience members before and after the circus to sell to them, as other practitioners did. Like his contemporaries, however, he did photograph performers who, in turn, sold their own likenesses to supplement wages. It is in this disparity between his desire to document and his need to earn a living that the most illuminating aspects of his work come through. With an eye on the individual story, Glasier could capture the mood of a circus employee "out of character," backstage, rehearsing, dealing with the minutiae of the day to day, while still imparting the energy of the circus itself. There are no "grab shots" with an 8x10 camera. For this reason, Glasier's photographs appear deliberate and thoughtful, well-composed and personal, while still salable.

To meet his financial needs, Glasier cropped many of his photos in a traditional manner, but the information outside these marks is equally interesting to the contemporary viewer. For instance, in "The Marvells" (page 51), the buying public would see the acrobats posing for the camera. Looking beyond the print that would have been sold by the performers, we see an unaware employee tending to a pile of equipment. Examining the whole negative in relation to Glasier's own crop marks, we are shown not only both sides of the circus, but both sides of the photographer. Glasier's work was unique in many ways, not least of which was the off-hand elegance he allowed his subjects. The performers all seem remarkably composed and relaxed in front of this photographer, which was, no doubt, the result of a mixture of personality and perseverance.

Glasier's photographic accomplishments have been largely overlooked by photo historians, but circus historians have long felt that he was among the finest photographers the circus has ever known. Other luminaries in this rarefied realm include H. A. Atwell of Chicago, San Antonio's E. O. Goldbeck, and Edward J. Kelty and his Century Flashlight Photographers. The collection of photographs presented here offers a tantalizing glimpse into the public and private worlds of the circus performers in the first third of the twentieth century. Through the magic of the circus, human and animal performers from the far reaches of the globe joined together to create a splendid diversion for an enthusiastic public. As a sustained document of circus life at this time, there is no known equivalent.

A WORD ABOUT THE PHOTOGRAPHS:

In a letter written by his wife after his death, Glaser is described as being a bit of an equipment hound, owning three 8x10 King View cameras with an accessory Thornton-Pickard focal plane shutter speeded up to 1/3000 of a second attached, Goertz lenses ("the finest obtainable"), Dagors for his 8x10 and "post card Kodak," plus a 5x7 Graflex rigged with a Coerz Celor and accordion-line focusing hood. Glasier worked with gelatin dry plate negatives, which were then commercially available. There are numbers on many of the photographs. We assume that this was either Glasier's own identification system or a system devised by subsequent owners of the negatives. The words on the edges of the negatives are almost certainly in Glasier's handwriting, meant for identification. The writing appears "backwards" because Glasier literally scratched the emulsion from the negative. For the text to be "right reading," Glasier would have had to write in reverse on the negative—a trick he learned for signing his own name on several plates, along with the names of a few performers. Whenever possible, the prints have been left full frame, allowing the borders of the images to be seen as they originally appeared. The titles of the photographs are taken from Glasier's handwriting on the edge of each glass plate.

Glasier's negatives are now owned by the John and Mable Ringling Museum of Art in Sarasota, in affiliation with Florida State University. The prints reproduced in this book were made from the original glass plate negatives and are from a private collection. Using circus route books, newspaper articles, obituaries, and old timers' memories, we have given as much information on each performer as possible.

Sells Floto
1923   #1

Unloading Wagons and Elephants Sells Floto Circus, 1923

The 1923 season opened in late March in Chicago and closed thirty weeks later in Cape Girardeau, Missouri, after doing 186 show dates and traveling 10,707 miles. That year was the first big tour made by Sells Floto to New England. The show featured the spec show "A Night in Persia." Notable performers include the Ward Sisters aerial troupe and equestrian director Fred Ledgett. Erma Ward fell during her act in Lowell, Massachusetts, but was saved by other members of the cast.

Hungarians on Parade Wagon, Barnum & Bailey Circus, 1903

As early as the third century B.C. parade wagons appeared in the chariot processions in the Roman Coliseum for the Circus Maximus. Historians attribute the rising success of the Circus Street parade in the United States during the late 1800s in part to the inclusion of fancifully decorated wagons brought over from Europe by Seth B. Hayes. The first circus wagons in America featured biblical, mythological and landscape scenes in wooden bas-relief. With the end of the last street parades in the 1930s, wagon-building and decoration became a lost art.

◄ Circus Trains Unloading

Early American circuses transported stock, baggage, personnel, and equipment in heavy, functional, plain wagons made of oak, maple, or hickory. The vehicles were numbered for practical reasons, but the numbering was not always sequential, to exaggerate the size and status of a circus. Once the circus went on the rails in 1869, pioneer Dan Costello came up with inumerable innovations that transformed the manner in which the show traveled. In 1872, W. C. Coup invented the crossover plate—a bridge-like apparatus which connected all of the flatcars in a continual runway, ushering in a revolutionary method of end-loading packed wagons.

RB&BB #1
1923

RINGLING BROS. BARNUM & BAILEY #1, 1923

While both African and Asian elephants have appeared in circuses, the Asian elephant is considered easiest to maintain in captivity. There are many ways to differentiate between the two. The easiest of all is by comparing their ears: Asian elephants' ears are smaller than those of African elephants. The trunk of the elephant also differs between the types, as the Asian elephant has one grasping "finger" on the end of its trunk, while African elephants have two. For circus performers, the hair of an elephant was regarded as being lucky, regardless of the animal's origin.

SWAN BAND WAGON LINING UP FOR THE STREET PARADE

Graceful and stunning, this huge bandwagon was built in 1904 by the Moeller Brothers of Baraboo, Wisconsin, for their cousins the Ringlings. The carvings were done by Milwaukee Ornamental Carving Co., which later did fancy plaster work for Milwaukee's motion picture palaces. The inspiration for the woodcarving came from the figures that grace the fountain at the Palace of Versailles in France. The Ringlings used a 24-horse team on the Swan Bandwagon to impress the townspeople with the size of their show. The Swan served in the Christy Brothers Circus, the Ringling Bros. Circus, Forepaugh-Sells, Barnum & Bailey, Ken Maynard and, later, at Disneyland. Baraboo, Wisconsin, was the Ringling Brothers' original home and served as the family's winter quarters from 1882 until 1918.

TICKET WAGON ON LOT, BARNUM & BAILEY CIRCUS
BUFFALO BILL'S TICKET WAGON NO. 3, 1906

Buffalo Bill's Wild West Show and its founder Bill Cody were living legends. After the demise of the man and his show, the legend carried on, a remarkable bit of Americana.

This ticket wagon traveled with Buffalo Bill in Europe and all over the United States. Cody inherited the wagon from James A. Bailey, whose Barnum & Bailey Circus had been touring England and Europe for a five-year period between 1898–1902. Bailey owned a half interest in Cody's show and so a great deal of equipment from the Barnum show made its way into Buffalo Bill's inventory. The wagon then worked its way back into the Barnum & Bailey shows.

This ticket wagon was found on a farm near Rochester, Indiana, which was the winter home of the Robbins Bros. Circus. The historic wagon had an ignominious career as a chicken coop until it was salvaged by the Circus World Museum. The farmer sold it for $10.

RESERVED SEATS.
RESERVED NUMBERED SEATS .... 75¢
GRAND STAND CHAIRS $1.00
BOX SEATS .... $1.50 & $2.00
BOXES SEATING 6 $9.00 & $12.00
CHILDREN UNDER TEN AND OVER FOUR YEARS
HALF PRICE TO CHAIRS AND BOX SEATS.
_____ TO NUMBERED SEATS.

BEWARE OF PICKPOCKETS

BEWARE OF PICKPOCKETS.

BARNUM & BAILEY
GREATEST SHOW ON EARTH.
THE
WORLD'S LARGEST, GRANDEST & BEST AMUSEMENT INSTITUTION
CIRCUS
MUSEUM MENAGERIE
OLYMPIAN HIPPODROME.
U.S. NAVAL EXHIBIT.

TICKET SELLERS: "BAD SELLER, FEELING WOMEN UNDER SEATS"

The scrawl on the left side of the image (in reverse) gives this photo its title. One wonders if Glasier was hired to photograph these men in order to distribute the photos to other circus owners so that they would not be hired again, at least as ticket sellers. The Ringling Brothers were know to run a "Sunday School Circus," meaning that they demanded wholesomeness and scrupulous honesty of their employees. It is not known if this photo is from a Ringling show. Here, Glasier was demonstrating a bit of economy by using only half of his glass plate for each exposure. Apparently, these subjects did not deserve a full plate.

◀ SIDESHOW ENTRANCE WITH ZIP, BARNUM & BAILEY CIRCUS, 1916

The cry of the bally, or the ballyhoo in circus jargon, often baited visitors to step inside the sideshow while waiting for the big top to open. As pictured here, the bally often stood on a platform adjacent to the ticket boxes, where he started the Grind, a speech about the oddities and fantastic curiosities just inside the tent. Frequently accompanied by musicians or other forms of entertainment, the role of the bally was to disarm and amuse the waiting patrons in order to draw them toward, and hopefully inside, the tents.

Zip, the What-is-it?, on violin, was born William Henry Jackson and performed in circuses nearly all of his eighty-four years. Barnum, always looking for the salient feature, dubbed him the "Missing Link" between man and ape. Zip died in 1926.

SLEDGE GANG

This was Circus slang for the work crew which gathered in a circle around the tent stakes each morning to drive them into the ground. With sledge hammers the group took turns hitting the stake to the rhythm of a repeated chant. These stakes were often pulled up by the elephants in the show. Roustabouts, pictured here, were the lowest-paid workers on the lot. Their duties included setting up the tents, moving props in and out of the ring, and cleaning up after the animals during the performance. The more skilled roustabouts, known as "riggers," helped set up the mechanical apparatus for the wire walkers and aerialists.

◄ BLACKSMITH'S SHOP TENT

Circuses travel with three types of horses: performing stock, workhorses, and deadheads. Percherons, Clydesdales, Shires, Arabians, and Lipizzaners make up the most popular breeds of performers. Geldings are considered the most reliable, while studs are overly excitable and mares are prone to biting and wild behavior. However, circuses do not select horses that are too docile, as high-spirited horses make the best performers.

Dan Ryan (Clown) and Child, Barnum & Bailey Circus, 1906

The 1906 program, or "Magazine of Wonders," lists Dan Ryan as a "German Broad Face" (character) clown. The route book for the same season features a photo of Ryan and fellow clown Hughie Zorella working a jargo mule parody. The child getting a peek under the sidewall is unidentified.

PEDICURE FOR PACHYDERMS

Elephants, referred to in circus lore as "bulls," have been a part of the traveling menagerie and the circus since Captain Jacob Growinshield from Salem, Massachusetts, brought the first elephant to the United States on April 13, 1796. According to P. T. Barnum, "Elephants and clowns are the pegs to hang a circus on." Although elephants were imported from both India and Africa, the Indian variety are considered to be more reliable, easily trainable, and capable of learning regular routines. Most circus elephants are female, as the males are considered to be more volatile.

❮ MENAGERIE, RINGLING BROS., 1905

In addition to the usual cats and horses, circus animals have included such exotic specimens as hippopotamuses, giraffes, gorillas, zebras, camels, rhinoceroses, kangaroos, tapirs, gnus, cassowaries, emus, crocodiles, anteaters, hedgehogs, and even penguins. At one point, this display was known as the "Ringling University of Natural History – The Rarest Zoological Marvels in America."

SIDESHOW PERFORMERS
ADAM FOREPAUGH & SELLS BROS.
CIRCUS, 1904

Highlights of this gathering include (from left to right): seated at piano, Mme. Clotullia, the Bearded Lady; an unidentified fat lady; Unzie, the Australian Aborigine Albino; James Morris, the Elastic Skinned Man. Seated are Lionell, the Lion-Faced Man, and Jo Jo, the Dog-Faced Boy. Other sundry performers and an assortment of midgets are thrown in for good measure.

Adam Forepaugh & Sells Bros Shows
Season 1904

Glasier '04

THE MARVELLS, RISLEY ACT, 1903

Known historically as icarianism, the risley act involves one acrobat, lying on his back, foot–juggling another, preferably smaller, person. As evidenced by ancient stone carvings, the skill dates back to the time of the Aztecs. First seen in the United States around 1843, the modern version of the act is attributed to Richard Risley Carlisle, who performed throughout Europe, Australia, and Japan until his death in an insane asylum in 1874.

◄ ADAM FOREPAUGH & SELLS BROS., CONCESSIONAIRES, 1904

THE MARVELLS

Glasico '03

MISS LAURENCE ON HORSEBACK OUTSIDE OF TENT AND GIRAFFE JARGO

The giraffe wardrobe, along with the routine itself, is referred to as a "jargo." Jargos are any two-bodied animal costumes used to parody actual animal acts in the show. Usually, a clown dressed as an animal trainer leads the jargo through a series of tricks. The blow-off to the gag comes when the two clowns inside the jargo suit get fed up with the trainer's commands and eventually expose the fraud. The giraffe jargo is considered the oldest of the genre, probably because a real giraffe was so exotic and rare in early circuses.

GIRAFFE, 1906

Giraffes traveled in specially designed train cars to accomodate their height. While they are essentially untrainable as performing animals, giraffes have always been a popular draw in the menagerie and in the opening spectacle.

IRON JAW ACT

In this specialty act, the aerialist is suspended by biting down on a mouthpiece attached to a swivel. Originally made of sewn leather, the mouthpieces later evolved to plastic and nylon dental plates. Performers ran the risk of gagging or choking on either the apparatus or their tongues as they were hoisted aloft by riggers.

M'LLE OCTAVIA, SNAKE CHARMER, RINGLING BROS. CIRCUS, 1901

The snake charmer was usually a scantily clad woman who simply held up a variety of non-venomous reptiles for display as the "inside talker" described them. Typically, the act would involve the charmer wrapping at least one giant boa constrictor around her torso. Snakes were included in the sideshow as well as a separate pit show on the other side of the midway, offering the townsfolk several glimpses of the rare serpents.

MADAME SCHEEL, LION TAMER

GLASIER.

SELLS 1924
FLOTO.

Two lady riders — Dallie Julian and Linda Jeal, Adam Forepaugh & Sells Bros. Circus, 1902

Dallie Julian was one of the most accomplished bareback riders of her day. She was known for her daring somersaults on horseback. While injuries during performances were rare, fallen performers were carted out of the ring with the ringmaster bellowing "Bring in the clowns!"

❮ Sells Floto Band Portrait, Victor Robbins, Conductor, 1924

As circuses got bigger, so did the bands needed to fill the tents with music. Having a band of twenty to forty members was not uncommon for the big top circuses, with music being a key element to both the street parade and the performances. The first pieces of circus music bear the names of the acts that they were to accompany, such as the "Grand Zoological March" and the "Seven Elephant March" of the Forepaugh and W. W. Cole show and the Sells show, respectively. To take part in the parade the musical acts were broken up into various novelties, from marching bands to ladies' bands to Scottish pipers, so that as the parade progressed the crowd was treated to non-stop music. The air calliope, an automated orchestra operating much like a player piano and first made in 1908 by Italian-American accordion player Joe Ori, became the one instrument most associated with the circus. Barnum & Bailey became the first circus to use the air calliope in 1913, featuring it both in the parade and with the band under the big top.

TEE-WEE-HE-MA, PRINCESS WOOTONE KANUSKE
(ONE OF THE MITCHELL SISTERS), 1907

Native Americans were featured in the American circus for many years. Circusgoers were fascinated to be so close to these "fierce Indians," even though the ones traveling with the shows were, for the most part, actors in a grand Western drama. This woman was said to be related to the photographer F. W. Glasier "by blood."

CHIEF IRON TAIL, C. 1914

A star of Buffalo Bill's Wild West Show, Chief Iron Tail was a skilled actor and performer. He was a Dakota Sioux and among the models whose likenesses were used for the Buffalo Nickel. The Chief was also photographed by noted artist Gertrude Kasebier and visited her summer home on Long Island.

THE ILLESON SISTERS, ACROBATS

Emma Stickney

Emma Rezac, a premier rider, was the second wife of Robert Stickney, and trained by the noted equestrian director in the sport. She was known as the "Fashion Plate Equestrienne." In addition to her equine work, Emma was also a wire walker and performed a few aerial feats. She rode in the circus with her family until July 6th, 1923, when she died from a reported fall out of an open hotel window. Her husband died February 24th, 1928.

MRS. ISABELLA BUTLER, BARNUM & BAILEY, 1906

Mrs. Butler traveled with Barnum & Bailey in 1906 and 1907 driving "L'Auto-Bolide." The stunt, also called the "Dip of Death," was invented by the Parisian Carlos Alonso-Perez and patented in 1905 (patent #795,087). It involved a car coasting down a steep curved ramp, turning upside down while jumping a 40–foot gap, and landing right side up on another ramp. This photograph shows Mrs. Butler's outfit for the "Pageant of the Nations" spec.

COOCHEE

The *danse du ventre,* French for the bellydance, was also known as the "coochee coochee dance," "oriental dance," or "muscle dance." In the wake of the World's Columbian Exposition, numerous women performed the highly erotic *danse du ventre* on the stage. Not infrequently, these performances were halted by the police.

ROSITTA MANTILLA, RINGLING BROS. CIRCUS, 1914

Rositta is shown here in the regalia of the spec production "Solomon and the Queen of Sheba." Biblical themed spectacles were common at this time, and lent an air of legitimacy to the circus for the Sunday school set.

❮ AFTER THE SPECTACLE

In the early days of the traveling tented circuses, when shows used a one-ring/one-pole top (the center pole was in the middle of the single ring and everyone worked around it), a parade of performers, animals, and clowns that would open the show would simply be referred to as a "grand entry." As shows grew in size and format, wagons and pony carts would be included in the grand entry. In 1872, "P. T. Barnum's Great Traveling World's Fair" introduced the hippodrome track, which separated the front row of seats from the ring itself. It was on this hippodrome track that the grand entry took place. This eventually evolved into the big "Spectacles."

By the early twentieth century, there were anywhere from twelve to fifteen hundred people attached to larger circuses. With so many bodies, it became possible for management to stage enormous production numbers, putting wardrobe on just about everyone that could walk. The earliest of these "spec" productions were full-blown pageants, such as "Cleopatra," "Nero or the Destruction of Rome," "Joan of Arc," and "Solomon and the Queen Of Sheba." Unless his or her contract excused a performer from appearing in it, everybody had a place in spec—top aerialists, jugglers, sideshow characters, and even roustabouts. Early on, the big specs opened the show. Through the early 1920s many of the shows carried huge backdrops, curtains, and stage-like sets for atmosphere.

PHYLLIS ALLEN.

UNIDENTIFIED

RAY THOMPSON

In 1904, Thompson was featured as a "High School and High Jumping Horseman with Forepaugh and Sells." He moved over to the Barnum & Bailey Circus in 1906. He was said to exhibit uncommon elegance and elan in and out of the ring.

DOLLY JAHN ON ROMAN RINGS,
RINGLING BROS. BARNUM & BAILEY CIRCUS, 1926

Dolly was the daughter of perch pole artist Hans Jahn. She was among countless other show kids who hung around the biggest star of the show, Lillian Leitzel. This photo was taken in front of Leitzel's private dressing tent. She always had a set of practice rings nearby for warm-ups before her incomparable act.

ERMA WARD, SELLS FLOTO CIRCUS, 1924

Erma's parents were going to send her from Peoria, Illinois, to a music conservatory on the East Coast in 1920. That year, at age 16, she joined the circus. As the star of the 1924 circus she closed the show with up to 200 consecutive one-armed planges on Roman rings.

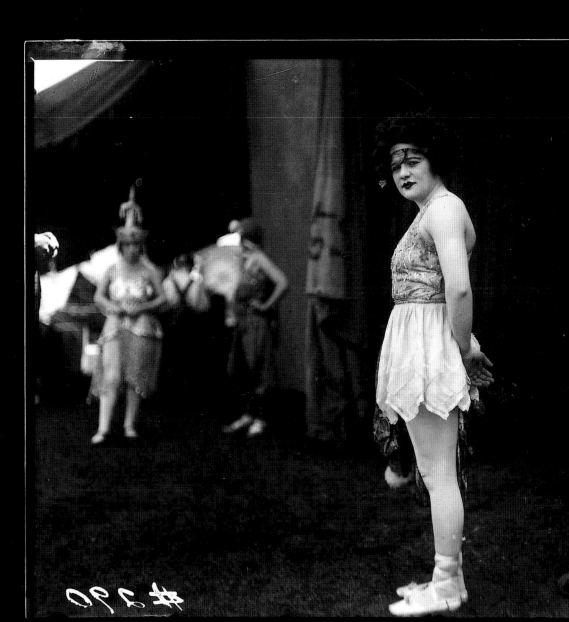

ERMA WARD.
1924.
SELLS
FLOTO.
#61.
Glasier Photo.

SPARKS CIRCUS, 1923

The Sparks Circus began as the two-car John H. Sparks Old Virginia Show in 1889 and was traveling on seven railroad cars by 1909. Due to its reputation as a well run and perfectly organized show, the Sparks Circus was known as the "circus man's circus." Sparks' son Charles sold the circus in 1928 to the American Circus Corporation, which then sold the show to John Ringling.

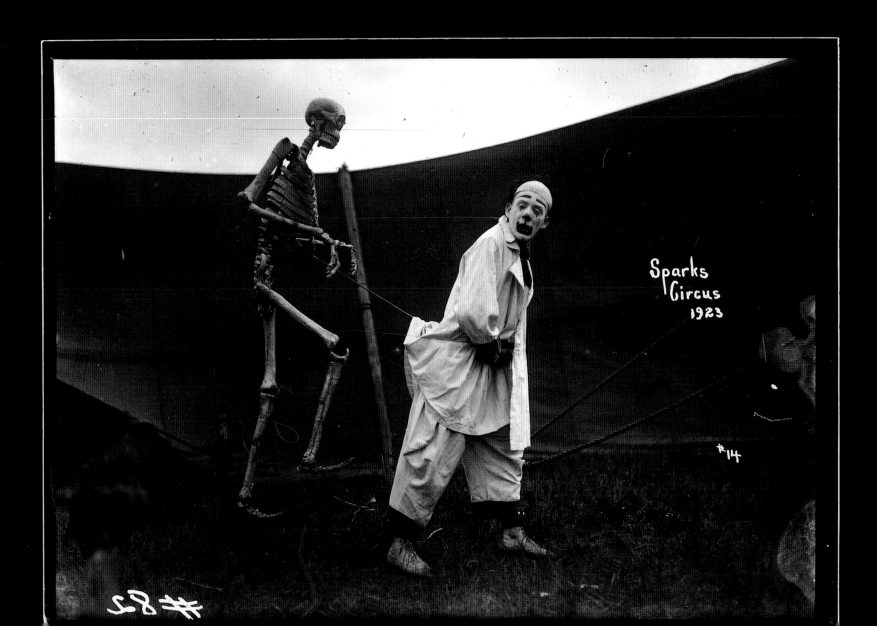

Sparks
Circus
1923

#14

FRANK "SLIVERS" OAKLEY & ALEX SEABERT, BARNUM & BAILEY, 1903

"Slivers" Oakley (left) was considered to be the greatest clown of the day. The tall Scandinavian was made a star with his one-man pantomime baseball game, which was reported to have been so funny that some of the audience required medical attention. He left Ringling Bros. in 1907 and went into "private practice." His behavior became erratic, and with the increasing eccentricity of his act he fell out of fashion. He asked for his job back in 1916, but was given only a walk-about clowning role at $50 a week—a far cry from his previous salary of $750 per week and a five minute solo performance for 16,000 spectators daily. A few days after agreeing to his new contract "Slivers" Oakley took his own life.

Oakley & Seabert

THE MARDOS, PETE AND FLORENCE

Pete Mardo, noted circus clown, was born Peter Guckeyson in Dubuque, Iowa, in 1882. He grew up in Akron, Ohio, and as a boy attended St. Bernard School. He started his career in the Sun Brothers circus, changing his name to Mardo when he began performing. His wife, Florence Harris Mardo, was a star equestrian. Upon retirement the couple operated the Tally-Ho restaurant and a tearoom in Ohio and belonged to the Firestone Country Club.

THE MARDOS.

CLOWN GROUP PORTRAIT

Traditionally there are three main types of clowns: the white-faced clown, the Auguste, and the character clown. Of the three, the white-faced clown is regarded as the most intelligent, and will often assume the role of ringleader in a group of clowns. On the other end of the scale, intellectually, is the Auguste clown, whose name is German for "fool." The character clown may dress up as a hobo, a rube, in female drag, or as a Chaplinesque type of tramp, to list a few options.

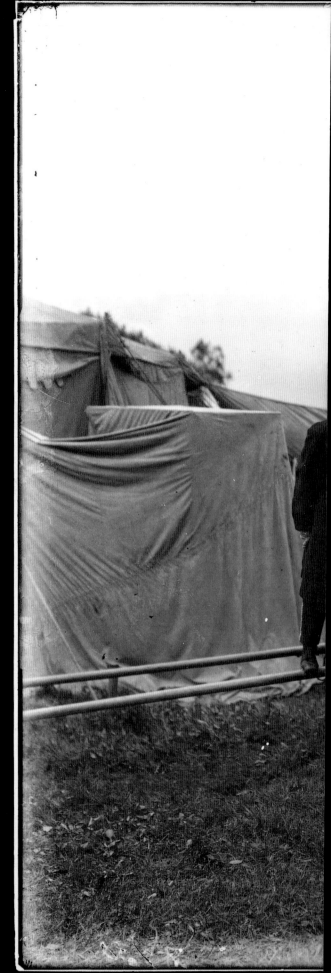

BLANCH HILLARD, AN ARENIC QUEEN, BARNUM & BAILEY, 1903

In this photograph we see not only Glasier's crop marks, but a bit of "sleight-of-hand" negative retouching as well. If you look closely, you'll see the ghost image of the handler's hand holding the steed steady.

AN
ARENIC
QUEEN

THE MEERS SISTERS, EQUESTRIENNES

The Meers Sisters (Marie and Ouika) were the principal equestrian act for Forepaugh and Sells from 1902-04. They moved to Barnum & Bailey Circus in 1906, where they remained a prime attraction for many seasons.

NAIDA MILLER, SPARKS CIRCUS, 1923

Naida was a noted tight-wire artist. The circus offered three types of wire walkers: slack-wire, tight-wire, and high-wire. On a slack-wire, the performer's body is the centrifugal force that moves with the wire. One of the familiar tricks on the slack wire involves the wirewalker swinging the wire back and forth with his or her legs, faster and faster, from side to side. The quicker the motion, the further out (to either side) the wire swings, almost like a pendulum, until the body is pitched in mid-air at a 90 degree angle. On a tight-wire, the body balances completely on top of the cable. The taughtness of the wire makes it possible to execute a completely different series of tricks, including jumps, somersaults and multiple-body pyramids. Finally, a high-wire is a tight-wire suspended high above the sawdust (and gaping mouths).

SIEGRIST-SILBON FLYING ACT, BARNUM & BAILEY CIRCUS, 1916

This has always been considered one of the greatest flying acts of all time. On the far right is Clara Grow, the woman who would become the first Mrs. Alfredo Codona. Cordona was the first to perfect the triple somersault on the trapeze. Clara joined the troupe in 1915. Also pictured: Marion Smith, Emily Hedder, Jennie Silbon, and Helen Bordner.

◄ THE FLYING FISHERS

Of all the circus acts, none held the attention of the audience more than the flyers, whose gravity defying spins and flips made hearts stand still. Here, against the gossamer background of the great tent, they appear as birds in trees, ready to fly.

EMMA STICKNEY, ADAM FOREPAUGH & SELLS BROS. CIRCUS, 1904

Miss Helen Girard.

Ella Bradna, 1928

Ella joined the Barnum & Bailey circus in 1903 while it was in London. While playing in Paris that year she fell from her horse out of the ring and into the lap of an Austrian cavalry officer who was vacationing in Paris. The two married and, due to Ella's fame, her husband, Fred Ferber, took her name. The man who became known as Fred Bradna was born into a family of brewers in Strasbourg. After he married Ella, Fred's father disowned him, and he joined the circus with his wife. Fred was promoted to equestrian director in 1915, a position he held for the next thirty years. He authored the circus book *The Big Top*. Ella performed as a bareback rider regularly until her retirement in her sixties.

ZELDA BODEN

◀ **WEDDING PARTY**

The social life of the circus was no different than any other small town. It just so happened that this small town was constantly on the move. Many circus people held their wedding ceremonies in the center ring in front of the spectators during intermission.

ZELDA BODEN

UNIDENTIFIED

MISS DeFORREST, 1904

This young trainer's family worked a dog and monkey act. Her father was also a center-ring strongman.

LOUISE DE MOTT (MRS. ROBERT STICKNEY, JR.) HANGING OUT LAUNDRY

Robert Stickney, Jr., was the grandson of legendary equestrian S. P. Stickney and the son of circus star Robert Stickney. Robert, Jr., was born on August 22nd, 1872, in Danville, Illinois. He married Louise De Mott, the famous equestrienne, in 1893. The couple had a son, also named Robert, who attended Villanova College, joined the circus, and received renown as a stilt dancer.

ALEXANDER PATTY, RINGLING BROS. CIRCUS, 1909

Patty was the best–known of a small breed of cranial hoppers—a brief fad that could only end badly. His agent claimed he could climb twelve stairs up and descend nine stairs. He worked for the Ringling Bros. Circus from 1907–10.

MIKE AND TOPSEY, AFRICAN ELEPHANTS, FOREPAUGH AND SELLS BROTHERS CIRCUS, C. 1908

Mike (a male) and Topsey (a female) were acquired together in 1878 and shown jointly for nearly thirty years.

MIKE AND TOPSEY

© 1908
F. W. GLASIER
BROCKTON, MASS.

BARNUM & BAILEY
GREATEST SHOW ON EARTH

MAIN ENTRANCE

Pay Day

EMMA STICKNEY, RINGLING BROS.

The primary categories of equestrian acts include "high school," or educated horse, also known as dressage, which involves a saddled steed that appears to perform without verbal or physical commands from the rider, who, of course, is giving imperceptible cues; Liberty horses — usually grouped by the same color — who perform riderless and without a harness; and bareback or rosinback riding, where the rider performs on the horse's back without a saddle and with feet powdered in rosin to provide firm footing.

❮ PAY DAY LINE OUTSIDE THE TICKET WAGON, BARNUM & BAILEY, 1903

Usually painted red to grab the attention of circus-goers, the ticket wagon or box office was often placed at the front end of the midway, the area near the main entrance that was lined on both sides by the sideshow, pit shows, menagerie, souvenir and food stands, and other attractions. Once a week the ticket wagon dispensed money to personnel.

Employees traveling with the Circus in 1903 would have included the cookhouse crew, animal trainers and keepers, roustabouts for the prop department, big top, and other tents, show personnel, management, cast and crew, banner brigade, bill-posters, lithographers, press agents, programmers, and the 24-hour men who checked the lots, the contracts, and the licenses to see that the billing was in good order.

Occasionally, the hired help of this period suffered the indignity of Red-Lighting, a slang term that referred to the abrupt dismissal of an employee tossed from the back of a moving train. As the person looked up at the disappearing train all he or she could see was the red lights of the caboose fading into the night.

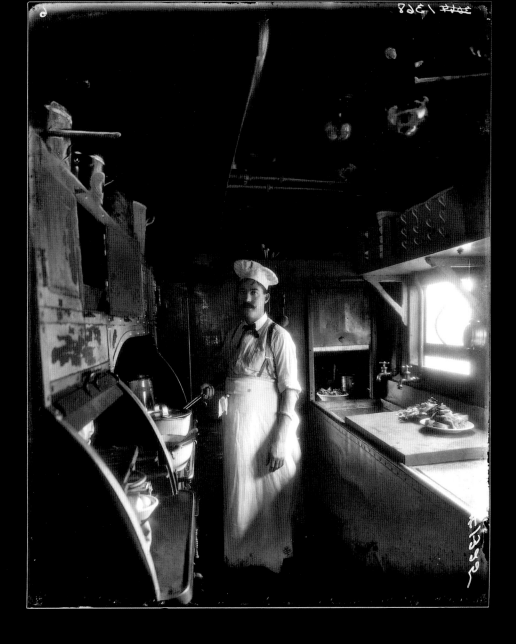

CHEF IN DINING CAR KITCHEN

The Barnum & Bailey Circus was the first to modernize the cookhouse for the traveling circus. Under the supervision of George Arlington, fresh linen, silver-plate flatware, and real chefs were all introduced, transforming the utilitarian cookhouse of the past into a gourmet restaurant on rail.

DINING CAR WITH GUESTS

nly star performers and top management were allowed to dine on linen, while the others on the show ate under canvas

The Armless Photographer.

⊰ CHARLES TRIPP, THE ARMLESS WONDER

Born in Woodstock, Ontario, Tripp was said to have excellent penmanship, and did not need assistance from others for anything save putting on his coat. He and Eli Bowen, the Legless Acrobat, were famous for riding a bicycle built for two around the hippodrome track. Tripp was also an accomplished photographer.

ACKNOWLEDGMENTS:

Many hands (and minds) contributed to the creation of this book. I'd like to thank the following people for their assistance and encouragement: Michelle and André Van Parys, Mara Sloan, Gay Burke, Jim Mairs, Anne Edelstein, Rosamond Wolff Purcell, Geoffrey Batchen, Tim and GiGi Tegge, Bud DeVere, Buff Ross, Gil Shuler, Valerie Morris, Andy Abrams, Alex Sanders, Lee Higdon, Roger Manley, Bill McCarthy, Fred Dahlinger, John Reynolds, Jonathan Gaynor, GeeGee Engesser, John Herriott and family, Stan Gray, Robert Bowser, Mark Lawrence, Tina Garrett, and Steve Lepre. The following institutions and organizations have been invaluable: the College of Charleston, Circus World Museum, The John and Mable Ringling Museum, Circus Fans of America, Circus Historians of America, Circus Model Builders, International, and Feld Entertainment.

SUGGESTED CIRCUS READING

The American Circus: An Illustrated History
John Culhane, Henry Holt and Company, 1989

The American Circus
Wilton Eckley, Twayne Publishers, 1984

American Circus Posters
edited by Charles Philip Fox, Dover Publications, 1978

The Art of Chinese Acrobatics
Wang Zhengbo, Foreign Languages Press, 1982

The Big Cage
Clyde Beatty, Century, 1933

Big Top Boss: John Ringling North and the Circus
David Lewis Hammarstrom,
University of Illinois Press, 1992

The Big Top
Fred Bradna, Simon & Schuster, 1952

Center Ring
Robert Lewis Taylor, Doubleday & Co., 1956

Center Ring Circus Cuisine
Linda W. Holdst, Cook Books, 1979

Circus: A World History
Rupert Croft-Cooke & Peter Cotes,
McMillan Publishing Co., 1976

Circus Days
Jill Freedman, Harmony Books, 1975

The Circus: Lure and Legend
compiled and edited by Mildred Sandison Fenner and Wolcott
Fenner, Prentice-Hall, Inc., 1970

Circus Heroes and Heroines
Rhina Kirk, Hammond, 1972

The Circus in America
Charles Philip Fox and Tom Parkinson, Country Beautiful, 1969

The Circus Kings
Henry Ringling North and Alden Hatch, Doubleday, 1960

The Circus Moves by Rail
Tom Parkinson & Charles P. Fox, Carstens Publications, 1993

Circus Press Agent: The Life & Times of Roland Butler
Gene Plowden, Caxton Printers, 1984

Circus Trains
Charles Philip Fox, Kalmbach Publishing, 1947

The Fabulous Showman
Irving Wallace, Alfred A. Knopf, 1959

Gargantua: Circus Star of the Century
Gene Plowden, Bonanza, 1972

The Great Circus Street Parade in Pictures
Charles Philip Fox and F. Beverly Kelley,
Dover Publications, 1978

Greatest Show on Earth
M. Wilson Disher, G. Bell & Sons, Ltd., 1937

Hoaxes, Humbugs, and Spectacles
Mark Sloan, Villard Books, 1990

Jungle Acrobats of the Russian Circus
Boris Elder, Robert McBride, 1958

Merle Evans: Maestro of the Circus
Gene Plowden, Bonanza, 1973

Mud Show
Fred Powldege, Harcourt Brace Jovanovich, 1975

Mud Show
Don B. Wilmeth, University of New Mexico Press, 1988

P.T. Barnum: The Legend and The Man
A. H. Saxon, Columbia University Press, 1989

Pictorial History of the American Circus
John and Alice Durant, Castle Books, New York, 1957

A Reckless Era of Aerial Performance: the Evolution of the Trapeze
Steve Gossard, Illinois State University Press, 1994

A Ringling by Any Other Name:
The Story of John Ringling North and His Circus
Ernest Albrecht, The Scarecrow Press, 1972

The Selected Letters of P. T. Barnum
A.H. Saxon, editor, Columbia University Press, 1983

Side Show
Max Rusid, Amjon Publisher, Inc., 1975

Step Right Up: The Adventure of Circus in America
LaVahn G. Hoh and William Rough, Betterway Publications, 1990

Struggles and Triumphs of P.T. Barnum
Warren Johnson & Co, 1872

A Ticket to the Circus
Charles F. Fox, Superior Publishing Co., 1959

Those Amazing Ringlings and Their Circus
Gene Plowden, Bonanza Books, 1967

Very Special People
Frederick Drimmer, Amjon Publishing, Inc., 1973

A Very Young Circus Flyer
Jill Krementz, Alfred A. Knopf, 1979

Yorkshire Gypsy Fairs: Customs & Caravans
E. Alan Jones, Hutton Press, 1986

Compiled by Lot 8 Manager, Circus Model Builders, International. Edited and amended by Mark Sloan

MINTING THE MARVEL, FOREPAUGH AND SELLS BROS. UNICYCLE ACT

GLASIER.